The Power of Focus

The Greatest Competitive Advantage for Increased Productivity & Success!

Gerard Assey

The Power of Focus

By
Gerard Assey

Publishing Agency:
Collection Skills
19/18, Palli Arasan Street
Anna Nagar East
Chennai - 600 102

ISBN: 978-93-92492-50-1

(Image courtesy Freepik on https://www.freepik.com- Thank You)

Contents

Preface

Welcome to **'The Power of FOCUS:** *The Greatest Competitive Advantage for Increased Productivity & Success!'*

In a world that bombards us with distractions and demands our attention from every direction, focus has become an increasingly rare and valuable commodity. In this book, we will embark on a journey to unlock the tremendous power of focus and discover how it can become your greatest competitive advantage in achieving unprecedented levels of productivity and success.

The ability to focus is not a mere skill; it is a superpower that sets apart those who achieve their goals from those who simply dream. Focus is the secret ingredient that allows individuals to accomplish extraordinary feats, make groundbreaking discoveries, and create lasting impact. It is the driving force behind the most successful individuals, entrepreneurs, artists, and athletes throughout history.

So, what exactly is focus? It goes beyond mere concentration. Focus is the art of directing your attention and energy towards a specific task, goal, or objective. It is about channeling your mental and emotional faculties to eliminate distractions and hone in on what truly matters. It is the ability to prioritize, persist, and perform at your best in the face of challenges and obstacles.

In this fast-paced and information-overloaded world, distractions have become the norm. We are constantly bombarded with notifications, emails, social media updates, and a never-ending stream of digital content. Our attention is fragmented, and our ability to focus is diminishing. But amidst this chaos, those who can cultivate and harness the power of focus will emerge as the true winners.

The benefits of focus extend far beyond productivity. When you master the art of focus, you gain a competitive edge in every aspect of your life. Whether you are striving for career success, personal growth, or creative fulfillment, focus becomes the guiding force that propels you forward. It enables you to accomplish more in less time, make better decisions, and tap into your innate potential.

Throughout this book, we will explore the multifaceted nature of focus and its transformative impact on your life and work. We will uncover the science behind focus and how it affects your brain, motivation, and performance. We will delve into the psychology of focus, examining the mindset and habits that separate the focused achievers from the rest.

Moreover, we will provide you with practical strategies and techniques to overcome distractions, build a focused mindset, develop productive habits, and enhance your concentration. We will discuss the role of discipline and willpower in maintaining focus, as well as how to tap into the elusive flow state where peak performance resides. Additionally, we will address the unique challenges posed by the digital age and explore ways to master focus in an era of constant connectivity.

By the end of this book, you will have gained a profound understanding of the power of focus and how it can propel you towards your goals and aspirations. You will have at your disposal a comprehensive toolkit of strategies and practices to cultivate focus and use it as your greatest competitive advantage. But remember, the real power lies not just in the knowledge you acquire, but in the actions you take. It is through consistent practice and application that you will unleash the full potential of focus and truly transform your life.

Are you ready to embark on this transformative journey? Prepare yourself to embrace the power of focus and unlock your path to increased productivity and unparalleled success.

Understanding Focus

We will begin by delving into the concept of focus and exploring its significance in our lives. Focus is more than just the ability to concentrate; it is the art of directing our attention and energy towards a specific task or goal. By understanding the different aspects of focus and its impact on our productivity, we can begin to harness its power and unlock our full potential.

The Nature of Focus: Focus is a mental state that allows us to filter out distractions and concentrate on a particular object, activity, or thought. It is a state of heightened awareness and engagement that enables us to channel our cognitive resources towards what truly matters. When we are focused, our minds become laser-sharp, and our actions become purposeful.

Types of Focus: There are different types of focus, each with its unique characteristics and applications. Let's explore three key types of focus:

- ✓ Selective Focus: This type of focus involves choosing a specific task or goal and dedicating your attention exclusively to it. It requires filtering out irrelevant information and resisting the temptation of distractions. Selective focus is essential for accomplishing complex projects, solving problems, and making critical decisions.
- ✓ Sustained Focus: Sustained focus refers to the ability to maintain attention and concentration over an extended period. It

involves immersing yourself deeply in a task or activity without being easily derailed. Sustained focus is crucial for activities that require prolonged mental effort, such as studying, writing, or engaging in creative work.

- ✓ Switching Focus: Switching focus entails the ability to shift your attention between different tasks or activities efficiently. It involves smoothly transitioning from one task to another without losing momentum or becoming overwhelmed. Switching focus is valuable in a fast-paced environment where multiple responsibilities and projects demand your attention.

Action Plan: Developing Awareness of Focus

- ✓ Self-Reflection: Take a moment to assess your current level of focus. Are there areas in your life where you feel your focus could be improved?
- ✓ Define Your Goals: Identify one specific goal or project where increased focus could make a difference.
- ✓ Single-Task Challenge: Commit to a single-task challenge for one day. Choose a task or project and dedicate your full attention to it. Take note of your observations and feelings throughout the day.

Understanding the nature of focus is essential to harnessing its power in our lives. By recognizing the different types of focus, embracing its benefits, and considering the factors that influence focus, we can begin to develop a focused approach that will significantly impact our productivity and success. In the following chapters, we will explore practical strategies and techniques to further strengthen our focus and unlock our true potential.

The Benefits of Focus

Focus is a superpower that can bring about a multitude of benefits in various areas of our lives. Focus is not merely a tool for concentration; it is a powerful force that enhances our productivity, decision-making, performance, and overall success. By understanding and harnessing the benefits of focus, we can unlock our true potential and achieve extraordinary results. Let's explore some of these benefits:

Increased Productivity: One of the primary benefits of focus is increased productivity. When we focus on a single task or goal, we eliminate distractions and maximize our efficiency. By dedicating our energy and attention to what truly matters, we can accomplish more in less time. By focusing on the most important activities and avoiding multitasking, we can accomplish more in less time. With focused effort, we can complete tasks with greater speed, accuracy, and effectiveness. Here are some examples of how focus boosts productivity:

- ✓ Completing Work Projects: When we focus on a work project without distractions, we can devote our full attention and energy to it. This leads to improved quality, faster completion, and ultimately, increased productivity.
- ✓ Studying for Exams: When students focus on their studies, they can absorb information more effectively, retain knowledge, and perform better on exams. Concentrated study sessions enable them to grasp complex

concepts and enhance their learning outcomes.

- ✓ Meeting Deadlines: By focusing on essential tasks and managing time effectively, we can meet deadlines with less stress. Focus helps us prioritize tasks, eliminate unnecessary distractions, and allocate our energy toward completing critical assignments on time

Enhanced Clarity and Decision-making: Focus has a profound impact on our clarity of thought and decision-making abilities. When we are focused, we can cut through the noise and gain a deeper understanding of the situations and challenges we face. By immersing ourselves in a task or problem, we can analyze it more effectively, consider alternative perspectives, and make better-informed decisions based on sound judgment. Clarity of thought and purposeful decision-making are crucial for success in any endeavor. Here are some examples:

- ✓ Business Strategy: Leaders who focus on their business goals, market trends, and competitive landscape can make informed decisions that steer their organizations in the right direction. By avoiding distractions and focusing on critical information, they can navigate complexities and seize opportunities.
- ✓ Personal Finances: Focus plays a vital role in managing personal finances. When individuals focus on their financial goals, track expenses, and make conscious spending choices, they can make sound financial decisions that lead to long-term stability and wealth accumulation.

- ✓ Problem-solving: Focused individuals can assess problems objectively, analyze available information, and consider multiple perspectives before arriving at effective solutions. By eliminating distractions, they can apply critical thinking skills and make decisions that address the root causes of problems.

Heightened Creativity: Contrary to the belief that focus stifles creativity, it actually enhances it. When we focus on a specific task or problem, we immerse ourselves deeply in it, allowing our minds to explore new ideas and perspectives. By concentrating our mental resources, we unlock our creative potential and can generate innovative solutions. Focus provides the space and clarity for new insights to emerge, leading to breakthroughs and originality in our work. Consider these examples:

- ✓ Writing and Artistic Pursuits: When writers and artists are fully immersed in their craft, they enter a state of flow that allows their creativity to flourish. By focusing on their ideas and honing their skills, they can produce works of art that are rich, original, and impactful.
- ✓ Brainstorming Sessions: In group settings, focus enables individuals to actively engage in brainstorming sessions. By concentrating on the topic at hand and contributing their ideas without distractions, they can collectively generate innovative solutions and creative breakthroughs.
- ✓ Designing Innovative Products: Focus is crucial in product design and development. Designers who focus on user needs, market

trends, and technological advancements can create products that address specific challenges, provide unique experiences, and drive innovation

Improved Performance: Focus is the key to unlocking our full potential and achieving peak performance. When we are fully engaged and immersed in what we are doing, we tap into a state of flow—a state of optimal performance and complete absorption in the task at hand. In this state, we perform at our best, effortlessly and with a heightened sense of satisfaction. By harnessing focus, we can consistently deliver high-quality work, surpass our own limitations, and achieve remarkable feats.

Reduced Stress and Overwhelm: Focus is a powerful antidote to stress and overwhelm. When we focus on one task at a time and break down complex projects into manageable chunks, we alleviate the burden of trying to juggle multiple responsibilities simultaneously. By prioritizing and focusing on what truly matters, we can approach challenges with a calm and composed mindset. Focus allows us to be present in the moment, reducing anxiety and providing a sense of control over our work and lives.

- ✓ Mindfulness and Meditation: When we focus on the present moment through mindfulness or meditation practices, we can calm our minds, reduce stress, and cultivate a greater sense of peace and well-being.
- ✓ Work-Life Balance: By focusing on work during work hours and dedicating quality time to personal pursuits, we can achieve a

healthier work-life balance. This balance reduces stress, promotes relaxation, and enhances overall life satisfaction.

- ✓ Mental Health: Focusing on self-care, engaging in activities that bring joy, and nurturing positive relationships contribute to mental well-being. By prioritizing these aspects of our lives, we can improve our mental health and resilience.

Enhanced Learning and Skill Development: Focus is essential for effective learning and skill development. When we concentrate our attention on acquiring new knowledge or honing a specific skill, we absorb information more deeply and retain it better. By eliminating distractions and immersing ourselves in deliberate practice, we can accelerate our learning curve and become experts in our chosen fields. Focus facilitates mastery and the continuous improvement of our abilities.

Action Plan: Leveraging Focus for Success

- ✓ Goal Clarity: Define a specific goal you want to achieve. Break it down into smaller, manageable tasks.
- ✓ Focused Work Sessions: Dedicate focused work sessions to tackle your chosen goal. Start with short, concentrated periods and gradually increase the duration as you build your focus muscle.
- ✓ Record Progress: Keep a record of your progress and accomplishments. Celebrate small wins along the way.

The benefits of focus are vast and impactful. Whether it's increasing productivity, enhancing creativity, improving decision-making, or promoting overall well-being, focus empowers us to unlock our full potential and achieve greater success in all areas of life. By recognizing these benefits, we can harness the power of focus and cultivate it as a valuable skill, leading to a more fulfilling and prosperous journey.

The Factors Affecting Focus

Let us try to understand the various factors that can influence our ability to focus. By understanding these factors and their impact on our focus, we can gain insight into the challenges we may face and discover strategies to overcome them. Several factors influence our ability to focus. Here are a few key factors to consider:

External Environment: The external or physical environment plays a crucial role in our ability to focus. A quiet, well-organized space can minimize distractions and create a conducive atmosphere for concentration. Consider these examples:

- ✓ Noise Levels: Loud and distracting noises, such as construction sounds or conversations in an open office, can hinder our focus. On the other hand, a quiet and peaceful environment promotes concentration and allows us to direct our attention effectively.
- ✓ Visual Distractions: Cluttered workspaces, visual stimuli like social media notifications, or a busy and chaotic environment can divert our attention and disrupt our focus. Organized and visually calm surroundings contribute to a more focused state of mind.
- ✓ Temperature and Comfort: Uncomfortable temperatures, whether too hot or too cold, can create discomfort and distract us from our tasks. Maintaining a comfortable temperature in our work environment promotes focus and concentration.

Internal Factors: Our internal state greatly impacts our ability to focus. Here are some examples of internal factors affecting focus:

- ✓ Physical Energy: Physical fatigue or low energy levels can make it difficult to maintain focus. Adequate rest, regular exercise, and a healthy diet contribute to sustained energy levels, supporting our ability to concentrate.
- ✓ Mental State: Our mental well-being influences our focus. Stress, anxiety, or overwhelming emotions can scatter our attention. Practices like meditation, deep breathing exercises, or engaging in activities that bring us joy can help create a calm and focused mental state.
- ✓ Mindset: Our mindset and attitude towards focus can either empower or hinder us. Cultivating a growth mindset, adopting a positive attitude, and believing in our ability to focus can enhance our performance.
- ✓ Health and Nutrition: Physical health and nutrition have a direct impact on our cognitive abilities. Poor nutrition or certain medical conditions can impair focus. A balanced diet, proper hydration, and taking care of our overall health support optimal focus and mental clarity.

Internal Thoughts and Beliefs: Our thoughts and beliefs shape our focus. Consider these examples:

- ✓ Self-Doubt: When we doubt our abilities or have a fear of failure, it can hinder our focus. Developing self-confidence and cultivating a positive mindset can help overcome self-doubt and strengthen our focus.

- ✓ Lack of Clarity and Purpose: When we lack clarity about our goals or purpose, it becomes challenging to focus. Defining clear objectives and understanding our purpose provides a sense of direction, enabling us to channel our focus towards meaningful endeavors.
- ✓ Negative Self-Talk: Negative self-talk and limiting beliefs can sabotage our focus. Practicing positive affirmations, reframing negative thoughts, and cultivating self-compassion support a positive mindset that enhances focus.
- ✓ Habits: Our habits shape our ability to focus. Building habits such as setting specific goals, managing time effectively, and minimizing multitasking can enhance our focus and productivity.

Digital Distractions: In the digital age, numerous digital distractions can impact our focus. Consider these examples:

- ✓ Social Media: Endless scrolling on social media platforms can consume our attention and divert focus from important tasks. Implementing designated time blocks for social media usage or using website blockers can help manage this distraction.
- ✓ Email and Notifications: Constant email notifications or smartphone alerts can interrupt our focus. Setting specific times to check and respond to emails, turning off non-essential notifications, and utilizing productivity apps to manage distractions can improve focus.
- ✓ Multitasking: Attempting to multitask by switching between different digital tasks can

reduce focus and productivity. Focusing on one task at a time and utilizing productivity techniques like time blocking can help combat the urge to multitask.

Action Plan: Identifying and Managing Focus Factors

- ✓ Environment Audit: Evaluate your workspace or study area. Identify potential distractions and make changes to create a more focused environment.
- ✓ Well-Being Check: Assess your physical and mental well-being. Set aside time for regular exercise, ensure you're getting adequate sleep, and practice stress-reduction techniques.
- ✓ Thought Awareness: Practice mindfulness for a few minutes each day to become more aware of your thoughts and how they affect your focus. Keep a journal to record distracting thoughts.

By understanding the factors that influence our focus, we can proactively address them and create an environment conducive to concentration and productivity. Whether it's optimizing our external environment, managing internal factors, challenging negative beliefs, or minimizing digital distractions, we have the power to cultivate focus and unlock our full potential.

Overcoming Distractions

Distractions are the arch-nemesis of focus, constantly vying for our attention and derailing our productivity. In this chapter, we will explore the common distractions that hinder our ability to concentrate and provide practical strategies to overcome them. By developing effective techniques to manage distractions, we can regain control of our focus and optimize our productivity.

Understanding Distractions: Distractions come in various forms, both external and internal. External distractions include phone notifications, emails, social media, noisy environments, and interruptions from colleagues or family members. Internal distractions, on the other hand, stem from our own thoughts, worries, and lack of mental discipline. Understanding the nature of distractions allows us to tackle them effectively.

Identifying and Eliminating External Distractions: To overcome external distractions, we must proactively identify and address them. Here are some strategies to consider:

- ✓ Designating a Distraction-Free Zone: Create a dedicated space for focused work, free from distractions. Remove unnecessary items from your workspace and establish boundaries to minimize interruptions.
- ✓ Managing Digital Distractions: Turn off non-essential notifications on your devices, set specific times for checking emails and social media, and use website blockers or

productivity apps to limit access to distracting websites.

- ✓ Establishing Communication Boundaries: Clearly communicate to colleagues, family, and friends when you need uninterrupted focus time. Set expectations and boundaries to minimize interruptions and create a conducive environment for concentration.
- ✓ Time Blocking: Schedule specific time blocks for focused work and prioritize important tasks during these periods. By allocating dedicated time slots for specific activities, you can minimize the chances of succumbing to distractions.

Managing Internal Distractions: Internal distractions, such as racing thoughts, worries, and lack of mental discipline, can be equally challenging to overcome. Here are some techniques to manage internal distractions effectively:

- ✓ Practicing Mindfulness and Meditation: Engaging in mindfulness and meditation practices can help calm the mind, reduce racing thoughts, and increase mental clarity. By training our minds to be present and focused, we can better resist internal distractions.
- ✓ Journaling and Brain Dumping: Take a few minutes each day to jot down your thoughts, concerns, and tasks. This practice helps clear mental clutter and frees up cognitive resources for focused work.
- ✓ Prioritization and Goal Setting: Clearly define your priorities and set specific, actionable goals. When you have a clear direction and

purpose, it becomes easier to stay focused and resist distractions that do not align with your objectives.

- ✓ Developing Mental Discipline: Strengthening mental discipline requires practice and consistency. Start by building small habits, such as staying committed to a task for a set period before taking a break. Gradually increase the duration of focused work as your mental discipline improves.

Creating a Conducive Environment for Focus: In addition to managing distractions, creating an environment that supports focus is crucial. Consider the following strategies:

- ✓ Organizing and De-cluttering: A clean and organized workspace promotes focus and reduces visual distractions. Remove unnecessary items, organize your materials, and create an environment that allows you to concentrate on the task at hand.
- ✓ Utilizing Noise-Canceling Tools: If you work in a noisy environment, use noise-canceling headphones or play white noise to block out external sounds and create a more serene atmosphere for focus.
- ✓ Establishing Rituals and Routines: Develop rituals and routines that signal your brain it's time to focus. This could include a specific pre-work routine, setting a specific time each day for focused work, or using specific cues that trigger a focused mindset.

Action Plan: Minimizing Distractions

- ✓ Digital Detox: Choose specific times of the day to disconnect from digital devices. Use this time to focus on important tasks without interruptions.
- ✓ Distraction Journal: Create a distraction journal. Note down instances when you were distracted and the triggers for those distractions. Develop strategies to address these triggers.
- ✓ Distraction-Blocking Tools: Explore distraction-blocking apps or tools that can help you stay focused during work or study sessions. Implement and test these tools.

Overcoming distractions is essential for cultivating and maintaining focus. By identifying and addressing external distractions, managing internal distractions, and creating a conducive environment for focus, we can reclaim our attention and optimize our productivity. The strategies discussed in this chapter provide a solid foundation for combating distractions and regaining control over our focus. In the subsequent chapters, we will delve deeper into additional techniques and mindset shifts to further strengthen our ability to concentrate and achieve remarkable results.

Developing a Focused Mindset

We will now get into the importance of cultivating a focused mindset to support our efforts in maintaining concentration and achieving our goals. A focused mindset is the foundation upon which we build our ability to direct our attention, overcome challenges, and stay committed to our objectives. By understanding the key elements of a focused mindset and implementing strategies to develop it, we can unlock our full potential and achieve unparalleled success.

1. Clarity of Purpose: A focused mindset begins with clarity of purpose. Clarifying your goals and understanding the why behind your actions provides a strong motivation to stay focused. Reflect on your values, passions, and long-term vision to define your purpose and align your efforts accordingly. When you have a clear sense of purpose, distractions become less tempting, and your focus becomes laser-sharp.
2. Commitment and Persistence: Developing a focused mindset requires commitment and persistence. It is essential to embrace the mindset that success is a result of consistent effort and unwavering determination. Cultivate a strong work ethic and a willingness to persevere through challenges. Understand that focus is not a one-time event but an ongoing commitment to prioritize what truly matters and see tasks through to completion.
3. Embracing a Growth Mindset: A growth mindset is a powerful asset in developing a

focused mindset. Embrace the belief that your abilities and intelligence can be developed through dedication and effort. Instead of viewing setbacks and failures as obstacles, see them as opportunities for growth and learning. By adopting a growth mindset, you approach tasks with resilience, embrace challenges, and view setbacks as stepping stones to success, all of which contribute to maintaining focus and overcoming distractions.

4. Practice Mindfulness: Mindfulness is a key practice in developing a focused mindset. Mindfulness involves being fully present in the moment, non-judgmentally observing your thoughts and emotions. Through mindfulness, you can train your mind to be aware of distractions and gently redirect your attention back to the task at hand. Regular mindfulness practices, such as meditation or deep breathing exercises, can increase your ability to sustain focus and resist internal and external distractions.
5. Cultivating Self-Discipline: Self-discipline is a crucial element of a focused mindset. It involves the ability to regulate your behavior, resist instant gratification, and stay committed to your goals. Practice setting clear boundaries and creating routines that support focused work. Develop habits that reinforce discipline, such as setting specific goals, managing your time effectively, and avoiding procrastination. The more you cultivate self-discipline, the easier it becomes to maintain focus and accomplish your objectives.

6. Positive Self-Talk and Visualization: The way we talk to ourselves and the images we create in our minds significantly impact our ability to maintain focus. Develop a habit of positive self-talk, using affirmations and encouraging statements to reinforce your focus and confidence. Visualize yourself successfully completing tasks and achieving your goals, creating a mental image of the outcomes you desire. Positive self-talk and visualization help to align your mindset with focus, enhancing your belief in your capabilities and increasing your ability to overcome distractions.

Action Plan: Cultivating a Focused Mindset

- ✓ Positive Affirmations: Create a list of positive affirmations related to focus and success. Repeat these affirmations daily to reinforce a focused mindset.
- ✓ Visualize Success: Spend a few minutes each day visualizing yourself successfully accomplishing your goals. This mental practice can enhance your belief in your ability to focus and succeed.
- ✓ Resilience Training: Identify a setback you've experienced and reflect on how you can build resilience. Develop a plan for bouncing back from challenges without losing focus.

Developing a focused mindset is instrumental in harnessing the power of focus and achieving exceptional results. By clarifying your purpose, committing to your goals, embracing a growth mindset, practicing mindfulness, cultivating self-discipline, and employing positive self-talk and visualization, you can develop a mindset that supports your focus and empowers you to overcome distractions. Remember, a focused mindset is a continuous practice, requiring consistent effort and dedication. With a focused mindset, you will unlock your true potential and pave the way for unparalleled success in all areas of your life. In the next chapters, we will explore practical techniques to strengthen your focus and enhance your productivity further.

Building Focused Habits

Building focused habits to strengthen our ability to concentrate and maintain productivity consistently is very vital. Habits are powerful tools that shape our daily actions and behaviors. By intentionally cultivating habits that support focus, we can create a solid foundation for increased productivity and success. In this chapter, we will explore effective strategies for building focus habits that will empower us to thrive in our personal and professional lives.

1. Start with Keystone Habits: Keystone habits are foundational habits that have a positive ripple effect on other areas of our lives. Identify keystone habits that directly contribute to focus, such as regular exercise, adequate sleep, and a healthy diet. These habits provide the necessary physical and mental energy to sustain focus and enhance cognitive abilities. By prioritizing keystone habits, you lay the groundwork for building a focused lifestyle.
2. Set Clear and Specific Goals: Clear and specific goals act as guiding lights for focus. Establish meaningful and achievable goals that align with your values and purpose. Break down these goals into smaller, actionable steps that are easier to tackle. By having well-defined goals, you create a sense of direction and purpose that fuels your focus. Regularly review and adjust your goals to stay on track.
3. Create a Daily Focus Routine: Design a daily routine that includes dedicated time blocks for focused work. Identify your most productive

hours and allocate them for your most critical tasks. Establish a routine that signals your brain it's time to focus, such as starting the day with a mindfulness practice or a specific pre-work ritual. Consistency in your focus routine helps train your brain to enter a focused state more effortlessly.

4. Practice Time Blocking: Time blocking is an effective technique for managing your time and maximizing focus. Assign specific blocks of time for different tasks or activities, ensuring that you allocate sufficient time for focused work. During these time blocks, eliminate distractions, turn off notifications, and fully immerse yourself in the task at hand. Time blocking helps create a structured and intentional approach to your day, minimizing the chances of getting sidetracked.
5. Implement the Pomodoro Technique: The Pomodoro Technique is a time management method that promotes focus and productivity. It involves working in focused bursts, typically 25 minutes, followed by short breaks. Set a timer for each work interval and commit to staying focused during that time. After completing a set number of work intervals, take a longer break. The Pomodoro Technique helps maintain a balance between focused work and rejuvenating breaks, optimizing productivity and preventing burnout.
6. Practice Single-Tasking: Multitasking is often seen as a productivity booster, but it actually fragments our attention and reduces efficiency. Instead, cultivate the habit of

single-tasking. Focus on one task at a time, dedicating your full attention to it until completion or the scheduled break. By focusing on one task, you can give it your undivided attention and produce higher-quality work in less time.

7. Manage Digital Distractions: Digital distractions can severely impact our ability to focus. Take proactive steps to manage digital distractions by implementing strategies such as:

- ✓ Turning off non-essential notifications on your devices
- ✓ Designating specific times for checking emails and social media
- ✓ Using website blockers or productivity apps to limit access to distracting websites

By consciously managing digital distractions, you create a more conducive environment for sustained focus.

8. Practice Regular Mindfulness: Mindfulness is a powerful practice for building focus habits. Set aside dedicated time for mindfulness meditation or incorporate mindfulness into everyday activities. Use mindfulness techniques to anchor your attention to the present moment, train your mind to notice distractions, and redirect your focus. Regular mindfulness practice strengthens your ability to sustain focus and enhances your overall well-being.

Building focus habits is a transformative process that empowers us to take control of our attention and optimize our productivity. By incorporating keystone habits, setting clear goals, establishing a daily focus routine, practicing time blocking and the Pomodoro Technique, embracing single-tasking, managing digital distractions, and integrating regular mindfulness practice, we create a solid foundation for sustained focus. These habits, when consistently applied, become second nature, enhancing our ability to concentrate and achieve our desired outcomes.

The Role of Discipline

Discipline is a fundamental component of achieving and maintaining focus. It is the driving force that enables us to overcome distractions, stay committed to our goals, and consistently put in the effort required for success. In Chapter 7, we will explore the critical role of discipline in cultivating focus and achieving our full potential. By understanding the importance of discipline and implementing effective strategies to develop it, we can harness its power to elevate our productivity and achieve remarkable results.

Understanding Discipline: Discipline is the ability to control one's behavior, thoughts, and emotions in pursuit of a desired outcome. It involves making conscious choices, staying committed to goals, and taking consistent action, even when faced with challenges or temptations. Discipline is the bridge between intention and achievement, transforming aspirations into tangible results.

Cultivating Self-Discipline: Self-discipline is the foundation of discipline. It is the ability to regulate oneself, make decisions aligned with long-term goals, and resist instant gratification. Here are some strategies for cultivating self-discipline:

- ✓ Set Clear Goals: Clearly define your goals and break them down into manageable steps. Having a clear vision of what you want to achieve strengthens your commitment and provides a roadmap for disciplined action.

- ✓ Develop Daily Habits: Build habits that support discipline and focus. Start with small, achievable habits and gradually increase the level of challenge. Consistency in daily habits reinforces self-discipline and creates a positive momentum towards your goals.
- ✓ Practice Delayed Gratification: Delaying immediate gratification in favor of long-term rewards strengthens self-discipline. Learn to resist short-term temptations and make choices that align with your goals and values.
- ✓ Embrace Accountability: Hold yourself accountable for your actions and progress. Seek external accountability through mentors, coaches, or accountability partners who can provide support and hold you to your commitments.
- ✓ Reflect and Learn: Regularly reflect on your progress and learn from both successes and setbacks. Use these insights to refine your approach and strengthen your self-discipline.

Building Discipline in Daily Life: Discipline extends beyond specific tasks or goals; it permeates our daily lives. Here are some ways to build discipline in everyday routines:

- ✓ Manage Your Time: Set specific schedules and allocate time for focused work, rest, personal growth, and leisure. Stick to your schedule and resist the temptation to deviate from it without a valid reason.
- ✓ Prioritize Tasks: Practice effective prioritization by identifying and focusing on high-value tasks that align with your goals.

Resist the urge to engage in low-priority or time-wasting activities.

- ✓ Avoid Procrastination: Procrastination is the enemy of discipline. Identify the root causes of your procrastination tendencies and develop strategies to overcome them. Break tasks into smaller, manageable steps, create deadlines, and eliminate distractions to minimize the urge to procrastinate.
- ✓ Develop Mental Resilience: Cultivate mental resilience to navigate challenges and setbacks. Embrace discomfort, learn from failures, and maintain a growth mindset that views obstacles as opportunities for growth.
- ✓ Stay Committed to Your Values: Align your actions with your core values. Make choices that reflect your values, even when they may be difficult or require sacrifice. Upholding your values strengthens discipline and integrity.

Harnessing Discipline for Focus: Discipline plays a crucial role in maintaining focus. Here's how discipline supports and enhances focus:

- ✓ Overcoming Distractions: Discipline helps resist distractions by staying committed to the task at hand and redirecting attention when it wanders.
- ✓ Consistent Practice: Discipline ensures consistent practice of focus-enhancing techniques, such as time blocking, mindfulness, and single-tasking.
- ✓ Task Completion: Discipline drives us to see tasks through to completion, even when faced with challenges or boredom. It prevents us from jumping from task to task, allowing us to

fully engage and concentrate on one task at a time.

- ✓ Long-Term Focus: Discipline keeps us focused on long-term goals, even when immediate results may be elusive. It helps us stay motivated and committed to the bigger picture.

Discipline is the bedrock of focus and success. By cultivating self-discipline, building discipline into our daily lives, and harnessing its power for focus, we can unlock our full potential and achieve extraordinary results. Discipline enables us to resist distractions, make intentional choices aligned with our goals, and persevere through challenges. It empowers us to stay focused on what truly matters and take consistent action toward our desired outcomes. In the next chapters, we will explore additional strategies to strengthen our discipline and amplify our focus for increased productivity and success.

Enhancing Concentration

The cornerstone of focus is the enhancement of concentration, Concentration is the ability to direct and sustain our attention on a specific task or object. It allows us to block out distractions, dive deep into our work, and achieve a state of flow where productivity and creativity thrive. By mastering the art of concentration, we can amplify our focus and unlock our true potential. We will look at practical insights and actionable steps to enhance your concentration abilities.

1. Create a Distraction-Free Environment: To enhance concentration, it is crucial to create an environment conducive to focused work. Minimize external distractions by finding a quiet space, turning off notifications, and eliminating unnecessary visual and auditory stimuli. Set clear boundaries with colleagues, friends, and family to communicate your need for uninterrupted focus during certain periods. Designating a dedicated workspace free from clutter and distractions will help channel your attention and optimize concentration.
2. Practice Mindfulness Meditation: Mindfulness meditation is a powerful practice to train and sharpen your ability to concentrate. Set aside a few minutes each day to engage in mindfulness meditation. Focus on your breath or a specific object while observing your thoughts and emotions without judgment. This practice cultivates the skill of redirecting your attention to the present moment and builds mental resilience against distractions. Over

time, regular mindfulness meditation enhances your concentration abilities in various aspects of life.

3. Use the Power of Deep Work: Deep work refers to the state of undistracted focus and intense concentration on a single task for a prolonged period. It is the antithesis of multitasking and allows you to accomplish meaningful work efficiently. To engage in deep work, set aside dedicated blocks of time without interruptions. Create a ritual to enter deep work mode, such as disconnecting from the internet, putting your phone on silent, and setting clear goals for the session. Embrace deep work as a regular practice to maximize your concentration and productivity.
4. Employ Time Management Techniques: Effective time management techniques can significantly enhance concentration. Consider the following strategies:

- ✓ Prioritize Important Tasks: Identify the most critical tasks that require your focused attention and prioritize them. Allocate dedicated time blocks when your energy and focus levels are at their peak.
- ✓ Time Blocking: Utilize time blocking to allocate specific periods for different tasks or activities. By scheduling focused work sessions, you can dedicate uninterrupted time to concentrate on important tasks.
- ✓ Set Realistic Deadlines: Establish realistic deadlines for tasks to create a sense of urgency and keep you engaged. Breaking tasks into smaller, manageable segments with

clear deadlines helps maintain focus and prevents procrastination.

- ✓ Use Productivity Tools: Explore productivity tools and apps that can assist in managing your time and enhancing concentration. Pomodoro timers, task managers, and website blockers can help you stay on track and minimize distractions.

5. Practice Visualization Techniques: Visualization is a powerful technique to enhance concentration and focus. Before engaging in a task, take a moment to visualize yourself deeply immersed in the activity, experiencing a sense of flow and accomplishing the task with ease. Create vivid mental images of successfully completing the task, feeling focused, and maintaining unwavering attention. Visualization primes your mind for heightened concentration and reinforces positive associations with the task at hand.
6. Incorporate Physical Exercise: Regular physical exercise has been shown to enhance concentration and cognitive abilities. Engage in activities such as cardio exercises, yoga, or brisk walks to increase blood flow to the brain and release endorphins that promote mental clarity. Incorporate physical exercise into your routine to optimize your cognitive function and improve your ability to concentrate.
7. Practice Active Listening: Active listening is a valuable skill that requires focused attention and concentration. When engaging in conversations or participating in meetings, practice active listening by giving your full

attention to the speaker. Avoid interrupting, stay present, and seek to understand the message fully. This practice trains your mind to concentrate on the information being shared and enhances your overall ability to concentrate in different contexts.

Enhancing concentration is a skill that can be developed with practice and discipline. By creating a distraction-free environment, practicing mindfulness meditation, embracing deep work, employing time management techniques, using visualization, incorporating physical exercise, and practicing active listening, you can significantly improve your concentration abilities. Remember, concentration is a muscle that can be strengthened over time. As you cultivate your ability to concentrate, you will experience increased productivity, deeper engagement with your work, and a greater sense of fulfillment.

The Flow State

In this chapter, we will delve into an important concept of flow state: which is a state of optimal performance and deep immersion in an activity. The flow state, also known as being "in the zone," is a highly focused and productive mental state where time seems to fly by, and our skills and abilities are fully engaged. We will look at the characteristics of the flow state, its benefits, and practical strategies to help you enter and sustain this state of heightened focus and productivity.

1. **Understanding the Flow State:** The flow state was first identified by psychologist Mihaly Csikszentmihalyi. It is characterized by a complete absorption in an activity, where our skills and the challenge level of the task are perfectly matched. During flow, our attention becomes fully focused, distractions fade away, and we experience a sense of effortless action and deep satisfaction.

2. **Key Elements of the Flow State:** To enter and sustain the flow state, it is essential to understand its key elements:

- ✓ Clear Goals: Clearly defined goals provide a sense of direction and purpose, allowing you to channel your attention and energy toward a specific outcome.
- ✓ Concentration and Focus: Concentration is vital in the flow state. By directing your attention fully to the task at hand, you can

block out distractions and immerse yourself in the present moment.

- ✓ Balance of Skill and Challenge: The flow state occurs when the challenge level of the task matches your skill level. When the challenge is too low, you may feel bored, while when it's too high, you may experience anxiety. The optimal balance stimulates focus and flow.
- ✓ Immediate Feedback: Immediate and clear feedback is crucial in the flow state. It helps you adjust your actions in real-time, maintain focus, and make progress.
- ✓ Altered Sense of Time: Time can seem to either slow down or fly by during the flow state. You become fully absorbed in the activity, losing track of time and experiencing a sense of timelessness.
- ✓ Enjoyment and Intrinsic Motivation: Flow is inherently enjoyable. The activity itself becomes rewarding, and you are intrinsically motivated to continue engaging in it for its own sake.

3. **Benefits of the Flow State:** Entering the flow state offers numerous benefits, including:

- ✓ Heightened Productivity: In the flow state, your focus and efficiency are maximized, leading to increased productivity and output.
- ✓ Enhanced Creativity: Flow nurtures creativity by fostering a state of deep immersion and allowing ideas to flow naturally.
- ✓ Improved Learning and Skill Development: Flow promotes accelerated learning and skill development as you are fully engaged and receptive to feedback.

- ✓ Increased Happiness and Satisfaction: The flow state is intrinsically rewarding and associated with a sense of fulfillment, happiness, and satisfaction in your work or activity.
- ✓ Reduced Stress and Anxiety: Flow provides a sense of calm and immersion that can alleviate stress and anxiety, allowing you to perform at your best.

4. **Strategies to Cultivate the Flow State:** While the flow state is a spontaneous experience, there are strategies to cultivate and increase the likelihood of entering this state:

- ✓ Identify Flow-Inducing Activities: Identify activities that naturally captivate your attention and evoke a sense of joy and fulfillment. Engaging in these activities increases the chances of entering the flow state.
- ✓ Set Clear Goals and Challenges: Set clear, achievable goals that align with your skills and interests. Strive to find a balance between the challenge level and your abilities to maintain engagement and focus.
- ✓ Minimize Distractions: Create a distraction-free environment by eliminating external interruptions and turning off notifications. Designate a dedicated space and time for your flow-inducing activities.
- ✓ Deep Work and Time Blocking: Incorporate deep work practices and time blocking techniques to allocate focused periods for your flow-inducing tasks. Establish a rhythm

and routine that allows you to enter the flow state more consistently.

- ✓ Seek Feedback and Adjust: Actively seek feedback to understand how you can improve and refine your performance. Use feedback as an opportunity to adjust your approach and deepen your engagement.
- ✓ Cultivate Mindfulness: Practice mindfulness meditation to develop present-moment awareness and improve your ability to sustain focus. Mindfulness cultivates the mental clarity and self-awareness necessary for entering the flow state.
- ✓ Embrace Challenges and Take Risks: Embrace challenges that push you outside your comfort zone. Taking calculated risks and embracing new experiences can lead to growth and increased opportunities for flow.

The flow state is a state of optimal performance characterized by intense focus, deep immersion, and a sense of effortless action. By understanding the key elements of the flow state and implementing strategies to cultivate it, you can tap into your full potential, enhance productivity, creativity, and overall satisfaction in your work and activities. Remember, the flow state is a dynamic and ever-evolving experience, and with practice and intention, you can increase your ability to enter and sustain this state of heightened focus and performance.

Key Exercises and Activities to Practice Being Focused

Here are some key exercises and activities that can help you practice and improve your focus:

1. Mindfulness Meditation: Engage in regular mindfulness meditation sessions to train your mind to stay present and focused. Start with short sessions, focusing on your breath or bodily sensations. Gradually increase the duration as you become more comfortable.
2. Deep Work Sessions: Set aside dedicated periods of time for deep work, where you focus on a single task without distractions. Use techniques like the Pomodoro Technique (working in focused blocks of time) or time blocking to structure your deep work sessions.
3. Single-Tasking Practice: Practice doing one thing at a time and giving it your full attention. For example, if you're reading a book, avoid checking your phone or engaging in other activities simultaneously.
4. Sensory Awareness Exercises: Engage your senses fully in daily activities. For instance, when eating, pay attention to the taste, texture, and aroma of your food. This helps cultivate present-moment awareness and improves focus.
5. Journalling: Set aside time each day to write in a journal. This practice encourages focused reflection, clarifies thoughts, and enhances self-awareness.
6. Visualization: Practice visualization exercises where you create detailed mental images of

your goals or desired outcomes. Visualize yourself engaging in focused, successful activities, and achieving your objectives.

7. Physical Exercise: Engage in regular physical exercise, such as jogging, yoga, or strength training. Physical activity helps release tension, improves cognitive function, and enhances focus.
8. Reading Books: Set aside dedicated time for reading books, focusing on one book at a time. This practice helps improve concentration and expands your knowledge and understanding.
9. Puzzle Solving: Engage in activities like puzzles, crosswords, or Sudoku. These activities require sustained focus and mental effort.
10. Music Appreciation: Listen to instrumental music or ambient sounds to create a focused and calming environment. Experiment with different types of music to find what helps you concentrate best.
11. Attention-Building Games: Play games that require focus and attention, such as chess, Sudoku, or memory games. These games challenge your cognitive abilities and help improve concentration.
12. Breathing Exercises: Practice deep breathing exercises to calm the mind and bring your focus to the present moment. Techniques like box breathing or 4-7-8 breathing can be helpful.

Remember, consistency is key when practicing these exercises. Start with small increments of time and gradually increase as you build your focus muscles.

With regular practice, you'll notice improvements in your ability to stay focused, maintain concentration, and achieve greater productivity and success.

Mastering Focus in a Digital Age

In today's digital age, we are surrounded by a constant barrage of information, notifications, and technological distractions that can hinder our ability to maintain focus, so we will look at the unique challenges and opportunities presented by the digital world and provide practical strategies to master focus amidst technological distractions. By understanding the impact of technology on our attention and implementing effective techniques, we can regain control over our focus and harness the power of digital tools to enhance productivity and success.

1. **Recognizing the Impact of Technology:** Technology has revolutionized the way we work, communicate, and access information. While it offers immense benefits, it also poses significant challenges to our ability to focus:

- ✓ Information Overload: The digital age has unleashed an overwhelming amount of information, making it challenging to filter out distractions and focus on what truly matters.
- ✓ Multitasking Temptation: Technology encourages multitasking, but studies have shown that multitasking actually hampers productivity and impairs cognitive performance.
- ✓ Constant Connectivity: The constant availability of digital devices and notifications can lead to a state of perpetual distraction, interrupting our focus and preventing deep work.

2. **Establishing Digital Boundaries:** To master focus in a digital age, it is essential to establish clear boundaries with technology. Consider the following strategies:

- ✓ Create Technology-Free Zones: Designate specific areas or times where technology is strictly off-limits. Establish sacred spaces or periods in your day when you disconnect from digital distractions and engage in focused work or quality time with loved ones.
- ✓ Practice Digital De-tox: Regularly disconnect from technology for extended periods. Engage in activities that allow your mind to recharge and rejuvenate, such as spending time in nature, reading a physical book, or engaging in hobbies that don't involve screens.
- ✓ Set Appropriate Notifications: Take control of your notifications and minimize their impact on your focus. Disable non-essential notifications and customize the settings to receive only the most important alerts.
- ✓ Designate Focus Time: Allocate dedicated periods for focused work without any digital interruptions. Use tools like website blockers or productivity apps to temporarily limit access to distracting websites or apps during these periods.

3. **Cultivating Digital Mindfulness:** Digital mindfulness involves being intentional and conscious in our technology usage to prevent mindless scrolling and distraction. Here are some practices to cultivate digital mindfulness:

- ✓ Single-Tasking: Instead of attempting to multitask, focus on one task at a time. Give your full attention and energy to the task before moving on to the next. Embrace the concept of deep work and practice single-tasking for enhanced focus and productivity.

- ✓ Mindful App Usage: Be mindful of the apps and websites you visit regularly. Evaluate their impact on your focus and well-being. Consider removing or limiting usage of apps that serve as major sources of distraction and replacing them with more productive alternatives.
- ✓ Digital Clutter Control: Organize and de-clutter your digital spaces to reduce visual and mental distractions. Unsubscribe from unnecessary email newsletters, de-clutter your desktop and digital files, and curate a minimalist digital environment that supports focus and clarity.

4. **Utilizing Productivity Tools and Techniques:** In a digital age, there are numerous productivity tools and techniques available to support focus and time management:

- ✓ Time Tracking: Use time tracking apps or techniques to monitor how you spend your time and identify patterns of distraction. This awareness can help you make adjustments and allocate time more effectively.
- ✓ Pomodoro Technique: The Pomodoro Technique involves working in focused blocks of time, usually 25 minutes, followed by a short break. This technique helps break work into manageable segments and enhances concentration.

- ✓ Digital Productivity Apps: Explore productivity apps designed to enhance focus and manage digital distractions. These apps can block distracting websites, track time spent on tasks, and provide insights into your digital habits.
- ✓ Digital Note-Taking: Utilize digital note-taking tools to capture ideas, tasks, and important information in an organized manner. Having a centralized digital system helps declutter your mind and facilitates focus during tasks.

Mastering focus in a digital age is crucial for productivity, success, and overall well-being. By establishing digital boundaries, cultivating digital mindfulness, and utilizing productivity tools and techniques, you can regain control over your attention and harness the power of technology to enhance your focus and achievements. Remember, technology should serve as a tool to support your goals, not as a constant source of distraction. With mindful and intentional use, you can navigate the digital landscape with clarity, focus, and a sense of purpose.

Famous Quotes on Being Focused

Here are 20 famous quotes on being focused:

1. *"Concentrate all your thoughts upon the work in hand. The sun's rays do not burn until brought to a focus."* - Alexander Graham Bell
2. *"The successful warrior is the average man, with laser-like focus."* - Bruce Lee
3. *"The ability to concentrate and to use your time well is everything."* - Lee Iacocca
4. *"Focus is a matter of deciding what things you're not going to do."* - John Carmack
5. *"Lack of direction, not lack of time, is the problem. We all have twenty-four-hour days."* - Zig Ziglar
6. *"The key to success is to focus our conscious mind on things we desire, not things we fear."* - Brian Tracy
7. *"Stay focused, go after your dreams, and keep moving toward your goals."* - LL Cool J
8. *"The successful man is the one who finds out what is the matter with his business before his competitors do."* - Roy L. Smith
9. *"The successful person is the individual who forms the habit of doing what the failing person doesn't like to do."* - Thomas Edison
10. *"You can do anything, but not everything."* - David Allen
11. *"The first rule of focus is this: 'Wherever you are, be there.'"* - Jim Rohn
12. *"Success demands singleness of purpose."* - Vince Lombardi
13. *"Focus on the possibilities for success, not on the potential for failure."* - Napoleon Hill

14. *"The more intensely we feel about an idea or a goal, the more assuredly the idea, buried deep in our subconscious, will direct us along the path to its fulfillment."* - Earl Nightingale
15. *"Concentration is the secret of strength in politics, in war, in trade, in short, in all the management of human affairs."* - Ralph Waldo Emerson
16. *"The successful people of this world take life as it comes. They just go out and deal with the world as it is."* - Ben Stein
17. *"Focus is not just saying yes. It's saying no to all but the things that are most critical."* - Steve Jobs
18. *"Stay focused on whatever you want to do and don't doubt yourself."* - Jenna Ushkowitz
19. *"Concentration is the root of all the higher abilities in man."* - Bruce Lee
20. *"Success is not the key to happiness. Happiness is the key to success. If you love what you are doing, you will be successful."* - Albert Schweitzer

Conclusion: Embracing the Power of Focus

Congratulations! You have reached the end of our journey through the power of focus. Throughout this book, we have explored the significance of focus as the greatest competitive advantage for increased productivity and success. We have learned how focus impacts every aspect of our lives, from personal growth to professional achievements. Now, as we conclude our exploration, let us reflect on the key lessons we have discovered.

- ✓ Focus is a Superpower: Focus is not just a skill; it is a superpower that enables us to channel our energy and attention towards what truly matters. When we cultivate focus, we tap into our hidden potential and unlock the key to achieving extraordinary results. By immersing ourselves fully in the present moment, we can overcome challenges, seize opportunities, and make significant progress in our endeavors.
- ✓ The Benefits of Focus are Multifaceted: When we embrace focus as a way of life, we experience a multitude of benefits. We become more productive, accomplishing more in less time. Our creativity flourishes as we engage in deep, uninterrupted work. We develop a heightened sense of clarity and purpose, allowing us to make better decisions and take decisive actions. Moreover, focus nurtures our overall well-being, reducing stress and enhancing our ability to find fulfillment in our pursuits.

- ✓ Overcoming Distractions is Essential: In a world filled with distractions, mastering the art of focus requires us to be vigilant and proactive. We must recognize the various distractions that threaten our attention, whether they be external stimuli or internal thoughts and emotions. By implementing strategies to overcome distractions, such as creating a conducive environment, practicing mindfulness, and setting clear boundaries, we can reclaim control over our focus and direct it towards what truly matters.
- ✓ Developing a Focused Mindset is Key: Focus is not just a fleeting state; it is a mindset that permeates our thoughts, actions, and habits. Developing a focused mindset involves aligning our goals with our values, cultivating self-discipline, and embracing a growth-oriented perspective. By adopting a mindset that values deep work, perseverance, and continuous learning, we can harness the power of focus and propel ourselves towards unprecedented success.
- ✓ Focus is a Skill that can be Cultivated: While focus may come more naturally to some individuals, it is a skill that can be cultivated and strengthened over time. Through consistent practice, incorporating focus-enhancing techniques into our daily lives, and maintaining a commitment to self-improvement, we can gradually enhance our ability to focus. Like any skill, it requires patience, discipline, and perseverance. But the rewards are immeasurable.

As we conclude this book, I encourage you to take the lessons and insights you have gained and apply them to your life. Embrace focus as a lifelong journey and a guiding principle for success. Remember that focus is not a destination but a continuous process of refinement and growth.

In the fast-paced and ever-evolving world we live in, the power of focus is more important than ever. It is the differentiating factor that sets apart those who merely dream from those who take decisive action and achieve their goals. By harnessing the power of focus, you possess the greatest competitive advantage in a world full of distractions and noise.

Now, armed with the knowledge, strategies, and inspiration found within these pages, go forth and seize the power of focus. Embrace the challenges, pursue your passions, and unlock your true potential. May your journey be filled with purpose, productivity, and profound success.

Remember, you have the power to shape your destiny through the unwavering focus of your mind.

Go forth and unleash **'The Power of Focus!'**

About the Author 'GERARD ASSEY'

Gerard Assey is a Graduate in Economics, a PGD in Management (HRD) and holds a Doctorate in Leadership. Gerard holds several International Qualifications in Sales, Debt Collection, Training & Teaching, and is a 'Fellow' of the prestigious 'Institute of Sales & Marketing Management'-UK, a Certified NLP Practitioner, a 'Certified Trainer', an 'Accredited Management Teacher-Behavioral Sciences', a 'Certified Competency Facilitator', a 'Certified Management Consultant'- (the International credentials of a professional management consultant, awarded in accordance with global standards of the ICMCI); and a Certification from the University of Michigan in 'Successful Negotiation: Essential Strategies and Skills'

He is also a Member of the 'National Association of Sales Professionals' backed with several years experience in varied industries, both in India and Overseas. He also holds an 'Etiquette Consultant' Certification from the USA (by Sue Fox, Author of Best Seller: 'Business Etiquette for Dummies'. She has trained some of the top celebrities' world over). He was also a recipient of a scholarship for extensive training in Japan on 'Corporate Management for India'.

Gerard Assey is 'Founder & Chief Corporate Trainer' of the Group: '**Citius, Altius, Fortius Unlimited'**- an organization that **celebrated 20 years of Glorious Service** in 2021, focusing on 3 Core Competencies:

People. Performance. Profit; in functional areas of Sales & Marketing, HR & Organizational Development, covering Recruitment, Training & Consultancy!

Having managed organizations with large Sales Forces in India & Overseas, his specialization cover extensive areas of Sales Training (All levels - Presentation, Negotiation, Key/ Strategic Accounts Management & Managerial Skills for all sectors), Bid Proposal/ Capture Planning/ Management Trainings, Retail Sales, Customer Service & Customer Retention Programs, Training for Prevention & Collection of Debt, Self & Personal Development Programs (Time Management, Teamwork & Team Building, Business Etiquette & Personal Grooming, Leadership & Managerial Skills, People Management Skills, Train-the-Trainer etc), including preparation of Custom-designed Business Manuals for Internal (HR, Induction, and Sales etc) & External use (Instruction, User Manuals).

Gerard has successfully conducted over 5980 Trainings & Workshops (as of Aug '23) all across India, Middle East, Africa, Europe & S.E. Asia. Besides public programs conducted regularly, both in India & Overseas, he has some of the top names as clients whom he services from Single Owners to large Public & Government undertakings, covering all sectors, for their in-house needs.

His website: www.CollectionSkills.com is the only one in this part of the world to be featured in the 'Collections & Credit Risk Magazine-USA' under 'Who's Who in Training' and ranks TOP, along with other websites listed below on most search engines.

Gerard is author of 76 books already (Sept 2023),

A few of the business related books being:

1. Bite-sized Bits on Commonsense Management
2. Heart to Heart on Life's Principles'
3. How to become a Successful Manager
4. The Sales Professionals' Master Workbook of S.Y.S.T.E.M.S
5. The Professional Business Email Etiquette Handbook & Guide
6. The Professional Business Video-Conferencing Etiquette Handbook & Guide
7. Professional Presentation Skills
8. Exceptional Customer Service
9. Professional Tele-Marketing Skills
10. Professional Debt Collection Skills
11. The G.R.E.A.T. Sales & Service Workbook
12. Sales Training Advantage for Results (*The Ultimate Sales Training Manual to enable you stand out as a S.T.A.R.*)
13. CEO Daily Planner & Organizer
14. The Sales Professionals' Master Daily Planner
15. The Professional Debt Collector's Master Daily Planner
16. My Daily Planner & Organizer
17. MY EMERGENCY INFORMATION RECORD (Family Emergency & Peace of Mind Planner)
18. The Ultimate Therapist & Counselors Planner and Organizer
19. Building an Ethical Workplace
20. Managing Relationships at Work
21. Managing Business Meetings Effectively
22. Effective Delegation Skills
23. Goal Setting for Success
24. B2B Selling by Email
25. Professional Business Etiquette & Grooming

26. Dining Etiquette & Table Manners
27. Effective Networking Skills
28. Grooming, Etiquette & Manners for Teens, Young Adults & Future Leaders
29. Inter-Personal Skills
30. Get Ready, Get Hired!
31. Selling in a Recession
32. Effective Receivables Management in an Economic Downturn!
33. Real Estate & Property Sales Training
34. Credit Sales & Accounts Receivable Management
35. Selling Skills for Real Estate & Property Advisors
36. Take G.R.E.A.T. C.A.R.E!
37. Spa, Salon & Health Club Selling Skills
38. Selling Travel, Holiday & MICE Services
39. Selling Skills for Spa's, Salons & Health Clubs
40. Retailing in Salons & Spas
41. Selling Holiday, Vacation, Tours & Packages
42. The Power of Sales Referrals
43. Selling Luxury
44. Technical Selling Skills Financial Advisors Sales Training
45. Dealing with Burnout at Work
46. Monopolize Your Markets
47. Selling to Affluent Customers
48. Financial Selling Skills
49. *The Effective Manager's Guide: Key Skills to Thrive*
50. From Aspiring to Inspiring: A Guide for New Managers on the Rise
51. The Power of Focus

Besides regularly contributing to business & trade journals, including international ones such as the 'Creative Training Techniques' and the 'Sales News' of the U.S.A, He is also a member of several prestigious bodies & trade associations, having participated in many Conferences & Workshops in India & Overseas.

Prior to his last assignment of leading & managing a large MNC as head, Gerard had a 3-year stint in the Middle East as a Consultant with a leading British Consultancy Firm.

As the past 'Official Country Representative' for the International Business Award- 'THE STEVIES'-(the business world's own Oscar) for about 4 years- he ensured a few Indian companies that qualify for the same every year!

Gerard can be contacted at:
Email: training@Sales-Training.in,training@CollectionSkills.com
Websites:
www.Sales-Training.in
www.EtiquetteWorks.in
www.CollectionSkills.com
www.RetailSalesTraining.in
www.SalesTrainingIndia.com
www.ManualPreparation.com
www.TrainingWithPuppets.com
www.FirstContactAcademy.com
www.SalesAndMarketingRecruiter.com

Our TRAININGS & BOOKS that can help your team

- ✓ **Sales Effectiveness**: Selling Skills for any Sector: Service/ Logistics/ FMCG Realty/ Insurance & Finance/ Media/ SPA's, Health Clubs & Salons/ Key Account Management, Effective Negotiation Skills/ Bid & Proposal Management Skills/ Retail Sales Training: Any Sector (Auto, Jewelry, Clothing, Luxury etc)
- ✓ **Customer Service Skills**-Complaints Handling & Customer Retention
- ✓ **Debt Prevention & Collection Skills**
- ✓ **Etiquette & Grooming**
- ✓ **Leadership & Managerial Skills**
- ✓ **Self & Personal Development Skills**: Presentation Skills/ Effective Communication Skills/Business Proposal Writing Skills/ Problem Solving & Decision Making Skills/ Empowering Secretaries-The perfect PA! (For Secretaries & PA's)/ Effective Time Management/ Teamwork & Teambuilding/ P.R.I.D.E- **P**ersonal **R**esponsibility **I**n **D**elivering **E**xcellence

www.ingramcontent.com/pod-product-compliance
Lightning Source LLC
Chambersburg PA
CBHW062113160726
48282CB00026B/788
* 9 7 8 9 3 9 2 4 9 2 5 0 1 *